Bubbles Fly to Happyland

Gilly Gee

ACKNOWLEDGEMENTS

I would like to thank all those that inspired me, especially Rebeccah from Lowestoft Library who started me off on the path to publication, and to Jo who got me the rest of the way.

I would like to dedicate my poems to my grandchildren and my great grandchildren.

I should mention my illustrators: Rob Way, John Begley and JJ.

CONTENTS

BUBBLES FLY TO HAPPYLAND

Whenever you blow bubbles, that is, the
watery kind,
do you ever stop to think of wherever up they
wind?
If you wish to know the secret of where your
bubbles roam,
the next time you blow bubbles, be sure you're
close to home.
The colours of the rainbow will very soon
appear
in the image of a window, curved and
sparkling clear.

Through this coloured window lies a magic
world,
like a crystal ball, its mysteries unfurled.

Gently blow a bubble, let it light upon your
hand.
Look through the rainbow window, and you'll
see Happyland.
It's the land of all the fairies where milk and
honey flow,
talking trees, babbling brooks and whispering
green grass grow.

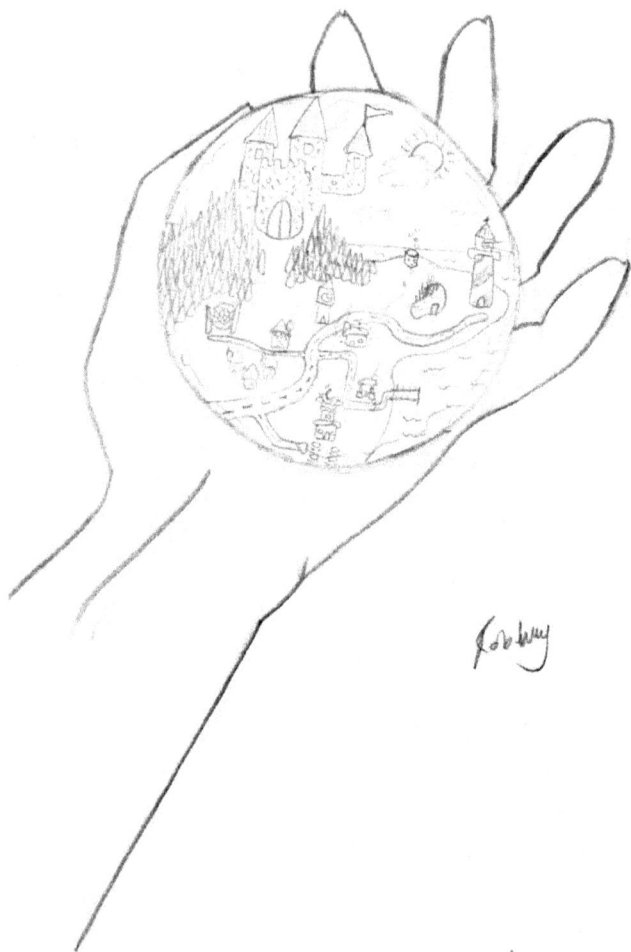

You cannot walk to Happyland,
it's much too hard to find.
So just blow up some bubbles, and don't you never mind,
as through the magic window there are fairies, elves and gnomes,
and lots of little people in their little people homes.
Unhappiness is not allowed. Should a bubble burst in tears,
it vanishes to Sadland, the home of dread and fears.
But bouncy, bubbly bubbles fly off to Happyland,
So give a helpful puff, and a gentle guiding hand.
Twirling, swirling, whirling, off your bubbles go,
up and down, round and round, dancing to and fro.
Away into the distance, until your eyes can't see,
they travel many miles filled with sparkling glee.

They come to rest in Happyland where bubbles cannot burst.

Living ever more afloat, these bubbles never thirst,
and never want for food, as hunger is not known
which is as well, as nothing's worse than a bubble overblown.
Bubbles have their duties to help the fairies out.
When fairies get too old to fly, they carry them about.
There are also baby bubbles, for fairy girls and boys
who haven't learnt to use their wings, and bubbles hold their noise.

Down floats a lovely bubble, what a large round globe it's made.
Look! There's the magic window, and there is Fairy Glade.
It's a little-people village, deep down in Dingle-Dell.
See the tiny fairy street and Wishing Fish's well.

WISH-FISH

If ever you wish for a wish to come true,
visit the Wish-Fish. He will help you.
Go to his home, where he lives in a well
On the edge of a wood called Dingle-Dell.

His well is quite deep, so call loud and clear,
"Wish-Fish! Wish-Fish! Please come up here!"
He'll swim up to you from his watery bed.
Watch carefully! Look! Up pops his head.

He wears a gold crown, as he is Fish-King.
Instead of bubbles, he blows a gold ring.
Catch the ring quickly in the little gold pail,
Shout "Thank-you, Wish-Fish!" He'll wave
with his tail.

Put on the gold ring, turn it three times round.
Think of your wish and don't make a sound.
If fairy bells ring, and fairy-lights too
flash on and off, your wish will come true.

MARY-FAIRY
THE QUEEN OF FAIRY GLADE

Mary's beautiful and kind with golden flowing hair.
She never has to worry about which dress to wear.
She waves her magic wand, three times more or less,
Then, hey presto! She has another pretty dress.

The fairies love her dearly and are glad that Mary's queen.
They know she will protect them from all that's bad and mean.
If danger should approach, she forms a fairy ring.
The little fairies huddle close, to hide beneath her wing.

When the danger's over, they flit and fly about.
Dancing and prancing merrily until the sun goes out,
then happily they hop and skip home to their beds,
knowing Bashful Badger will protect their sleepy heads.

PRICKLES SHARP
TRAFFIC COP

Prickles Sharp the hedgehog makes a point of law.
He is the village traffic cop. Mistakes he won't ignore!
Don't ever try to needle him or you will make him sore.

He always says, with caution, to slippery Sam the Snake,
"With your wiggly wanton ways, no one can overtake.
You must try not to wiggle, for everybody's sake."

He gives a written warning to poor Miss Millipede.
"Your feet have run away with you at an over-running speed,
To be footloose on a footpath is very bad indeed!"

Another time he caught the bees as they buzzed busily by.
He grabbed them by their stinging tails, which made them want to cry.

"You're dripping sticky honey about."
"Zorry, Zir" they sigh.

Sidney Snail glides slowly on, slow's all the speed he has,
"You're holding up the traffic, it really is too bad."
"I'm only holding up my house," grinned the cheeky slow-coach lad.

There was the time Sir Grassy Hopper jumped and jumped the queue.
Our traffic cop got angry. He said, "This will not do.
You know you should know better. It's a jumped-up charge for you."

Once a crane-fly overturned as he traveled over toad.
There are many other cases, in fact, an overload,
but Sharp's the traffic cop, and he's sharp upon the road.

MAGIC SHOPS

Fairy street has magic shops. Doors open by
themselves.
Magic carpets carry you to never-empty
shelves.
There are never-empty bottles that never need
refilling.
They also are returnable and do so for one
shilling!

For every item that you buy, another takes its
place,
as magic shelves in magic shops won't stand
for empty space.
Call the name of what-you-wish, and what-it-is
will glide
down into the basket hovering by your side.

Remember! These are magic goods. Think well
before you choose.
There's some will do the work for you. Look
out for helpful clues.
Buy Soapy-Suds, he'll do the wash, with one-
good turn from Tap.
Bristle-Broom will sweep the floor. He's such a
helpful chap.

Fatty's good at frying chips, fresh fishes gently battered.
They jump in with a fishy grin, so fish and chips are spattered.
Corn-Flakes a bit at breakfast. Puffed-Wheat is short of breath.
Poached-Egg on toast will fill you most, but is always cooked to death.

To get stuck in to strawberry-jam could be a bad mistake,
If no one's about to pull you out, it's a messy choice to make.
If you fancy cakes for tea, Self-Raising Flour will rise.
She makes a meal, and we all feel she's one of the best buys.

Once your shopping basket's full, pay the cashier gnome.
Tell the basket where you live and it will hover home.
Tea leaves in a hurry to join both cup and pot, so when you walk in through the door, tea's waiting, piping hot.

MR AND MRS DICKIE DORMOUSE

Mr and Mrs Dickie Dormouse
live under the door of a broken-down house.
To see who approaches their lying-down door,
They look through the keyhole, as that's what
it's for.
Should they be chased by Freddie the Fox,
They quickly jump through the letterbox.

With six little ones to clothe and feed,
they've employed the help of Miss Millipede.
She can sweep and dust and polish and sew
and cook a full meal and tie a neat bow.
With her many hands, the work's soon done,
so there's lots of time for having fun.

The little ones howl when she scrubs their ears,
but Miss Millipede knows they are put-on
tears.
When it's time to get up, they want to sleep,
such strange hours these dormice keep.
They yawn and stretch, then curl up tight.
It's no wonder they stay awake all night.

THE MICE-BAND

The six little mice
have a six-piece band.
The music they play
sounds loud and grand.
One plays trumpet,
another plays drums.
A violin for the third,
fourth whistles and hums.
The fifth plays a flute,
he's very keen.
Sixth dances gaily
with a tambourine.

MR. MONEY-SPIDER

BANK MANAGER

Mr. Money-Spider
keeps the local bank.
He carries out his business
in a disused water-tank.
He gathers up the money
and spins some wool from steel.
It makes a safe as good as gold
as steel wool is hard to peel.
All the fairies have great faith
in Mr Money's spinning safe.

In the bank there is a clerk.
His name is Adder Bill.
He figures out each total sum
with paper, ink and quill.
He never ever makes mistakes
and never takes away
any money from the bank,
except his take-home pay.
No one else could take Bill's place.
Who would try in an adder's case?

SUZY SQUIRREL'S STORE

Pretty Suzy Squirrel keeps the local store.
She bustles to and fro across her shiny floor.
Her tail curls up and over which tickles her
poor nose,
so Suzy Squirrel sneezes everywhere she goes

On her cap and apron are lots of polka-dots.
As she's such a tidy squirrel, I'm surprised
she's got such spots.
Not a spot of dirt or dust dares cross Miss
Suzy's path,
as with her mop and bucket, she gives them all
a bath.

When Suzy's fast asleep, her store becomes
alive,
between the hours of darkness, from nine pm
to five.
Jam puffs up her cheek and says, "Let's have
some fun!"
"We'll play tag!" shouts syrup, as he begins to
run.

Butter flies across the room to let the lettuce
out.

"I'll be it!" says cabbage, as he jumps up with a sprout.

Apple crumbles on the floor in her haste to get away.

Liquorice sticks his tongue out. "I do not want to play."

Brandy snaps, "You're very rude, and you have gone too far.

It's licking into shape you need. Get back in your jar!"

Lemonade pops up his cork. "I'd like to play this game!"

He jumps about and spurts right out, what a mess and what a shame!

Sausage rolls about quite puffed, as he is nearly caught.

Elastic band pulls up and says, "I'm feeling rather taut.

Let's stop this game before I bust!" and Ice Creams out, "Yes, stop!

I'm melting with this running game into the Soda-pop."

Orange squashes up his face: "I will agree to that.

It's getting very hot in here. Look at dripping fat!"

This made sticky-bun turn round. She's in a hot-cross mood.
"Through this silly game of tag, we'll all be gone-off food."

Sandwich spreads across the floor, curling on her side.
"Crumbs. I'm dropping everywhere! And crumbs I'd better hide.
Miss Squirrel's sure to find that I have left my tray.
Besides it's nearly five o'clock and the starting of the day."

BASHFUL BADGER
NIGHT WATCHMAN

Here comes Bashful Badger
creeping out at night.
Watching over Fairy Street
with his lantern bright.
He's the fairies' night watchman,
he wears a coat of black.
He carries tea and sandwiches
in a knapsack on his back.

When the hour of darkness comes,
evil elves and gnomes
and hideous hairy brownies
try to enter fairies' homes.
But brave and Bashful Badger
soon puts a stop to that.
He charges them with all his force,
and knocks them all down flat.

Creaky, crackly goblins
and naughty little imps,
love playing horrid tricks
on peaceful sprites and nymphs.
They'd best watch out for Badger,
if he catches them about.
He'll give them such a telling-off

And a heavy, well-earned clout.

Woe-betide any hooting owl
out for a midnight lark,
As Bashful Badger's eyes can see,
even in the dark.
He's kind, is Bashful Badger,
but he'll always shy away,
So, don't expect this night watchman
to pass the time of day.

ROY RABBIT

GREENGROCER'S SHOP

Each morning, in Roy Rabbit's shop,
he's busy sorting out
lettuces and cabbages
and occasionally, a sprout.
Bunches of red radishes
and orange carrots too.
Lots of healthy vegetables
to sell, to cook, to chew.
He used to keep crab-apples
but they always crawled away.
So, now he's stuck to sticky fruit.
they find it hard to stray.
Each evening, when his shop is shut.
Roy Rabbit rolls his sleeves,
as there's lots of litter on the floor,
cabbage and lettuce leaves.
Roy's tiny rabbit children
are the litter cleaner-uppers,
which saves their busy mother
lots of getting-ready suppers.
Roy looks around his tidy shop,
shouts "Goodnight!" to all his wares.
Gathers his little ones by the ears
and carries them upstairs.

SWIFT AND SWALLOW CAFÉ

I'm Swallow, he's Swift. We're brothers in
trade.
Eat at our place where our tables are laid,
with hot toast and crumpets and thick
marmalade.

Fancy cream buns, delicious and light.
Just made to your taste, so you take a bite.
As they float down inside, you're filled with
delight.

There's cup-cakes full up with a hot chocolate
treat.
Sugar-plum fairies, the sort you can eat,
and gingerbread men with edible feet.

Then swallow with pleasure, best fairy cakes
made.
Drink it all down with iced lemonade,
served with Swift service, the best in the glade.

Try upside-down cake served left to right,
or butterfly cakes. They're nice, but they might
fly from you hand, so you hold on tight!

Yes! Please come on in and do take a seat.

We're doing so well. We'll soon have a fleet
of Swift eating places so tempting and neat.

HERBERT SHERBET FLY

Herbert is a Sherbet Fly in Suzy Squirrel's store.
He buzzes around until he's found Sherbet Dabs galore.
"Oh good!" says he, "Just right for me. Large is my favourite size!
I'll take two, or perhaps a few," he says, with bulging eyes.

As Herbert leaves Miss Suzy's store, he clutches his bag with glee.
He thinks "I'll eat some on the way, the rest I'll have for tea."
Herbert doesn't seem to care that it is raining hard,
As he splashes through the puddles in Miss Suzie's yard.

If silly Herbert Sherbet Fly would only use his brain,
he'd realize fizzy Sherbet Dabs won't mix with watery rain.
He opens up his paper bag. The contents soon are soaked.
"Oh look! My lovely Sherbet Dabs, they're ruined," Herbert choked.

Fizzy, bubbly Sherbet Dabs fizz and bubble more.

Fizz and bubble, bubble and fizz, swallowing Suzie's store.

"Oh no!" cries out poor Herbert, as he tries to fly away.

"I'm all stuck up, I cannot move. I'll not get home today!"

Silly Herbert Sherbet Fly is rescued by the rain.

Pouring water soaks his skin, washing him clean again.

Says he, as he walks sadly home, his wings too wet to fly.

"I'll never eat Sherbet Dabs again!" He dabs his watery eye.

Rowley.

DAINTY DOZY DREAM-MOUSE

Dainty Dozy Dream-Mouse
keeps a Sleeping Store.
See her pretty flower-beds,
and puff-ball pillows galore.
She has mattresses of knapweed
and blankets of pure snow.
Bedspreads of red roses,
and sheets of ice that glow.

Soft eiderdowns of feathers
supplied by Duck and Swan,
are in return for water-beds
now winter's coming on.
In every puff-ball pillow,
sweet dreams are gently stuffed,
so when you go to bed each night
Be sure your pillow's puffed.

Spring is there in every bed,
so curl up extra tight,
as in cozy-dozy comfort,
you're cozy-warm all night.
Count lots and lots of wooly lambs
until you're fast asleep,
Then off to Dreamland you will go
on the backs of friendly sheep.

CLOCKMAKER KUKU

I'm Clockmaker Kuku. I make lots of clocks.
Big ones and small ones with on-time tick-
tocks.
I clock on in the morning and keep on the go,
my hands always moving, they never go slow.

I count every second on every clock face.
No careless minute dares drop out of place.
If I sleep on the job, they could come to harm,
so I've built in each one a wake-me alarm!

In the passage of time, standing guard by the
wall,
is a Grandfather clock so stately and tall.
He puts all his weight in his pendulum swing.
He sounds a loud dong, because he can't ding.

Grandmother clock, trying hard not to smile
hides her face with her hands, as she watches
his dial.
As nighttime draws near, the small clocks go
slow.
"Now just wait a minute! It's not time to go!"

But hours have flown past and time's run
away,

so my tired hands stop at the end of the day.
I clock out at night on the five o'clock chime,
and wind up at home at my regular time.

WICKED WILLIE AND SLY SIDNEY

Wicked Willie Weasel and Sidney Sly Stoat
are teasing poor Roy Rabbit. They grab him by
his coat.
He thumps his feet in anger. They twist and
turn him round.
"Stop! Stop!" cries out poor Rabbit, as he falls
upon the ground.
Up again they drag him, they twist and turn
him more.
"Ha! Ha!" they laugh and call him names
As he slumps down to the floor!
"Come on!" says Sly Sidney. "More mischief
we can do.
This shop is far too neat for me. Is it too neat
for you?"
"Oh, yes!" says Wicked Willie. "It will not do
at all.
Untidiness is more my game. Come on. Let's
have a ball!"
Crash! and Bang! and Wallop! Oh! What a
sorry sight,
As boxes break across the floor and vegetables
take flight.

"Squelch! Squelch!" cries Ripe Tomato, as her
skin begins to split.

"Crunch! Crunch!" cries Orange Carrot. "I think I've lost a bit."
"I've lost a stone already," says a sweet and tasty Date.
"Roy Rabbit will not sell me if I am underweight."
"We're black and blue all over and berry, berry squashed,"
groaned Raspberry and Strawberry, "and we have just been washed."

"I'm scared!" says Hairy Gooseberry. "I've goose-pimples all around!"
"And what of me?" says Onion Leek. "I've leaked upon the ground."

"I'm sour, and bitter too. It's all too much to bear.
These wicked creatures must be stopped," says under-ripe Green Pear.
"I'll run for help the quickest," said helpful Runner-Bean.
"I'll bring back Prickles Sharp and Mary Fairy Queen."

Runner-Bean runs very fast, hollering as he goes.

He's run and been and back again, before you count your toes.
By his side are Mary, and Prickles Sharp the cop.
They look about in anger, around Roy Rabbit's shop.
Their eyes cannot believe the chaos lying there.
Wilting fruit and vegetables, drooping with despair.

"Well! What's all this?" cries Mary. "What is this awful din?
Don't you know that being bad is a fairy naughty sin?!'
She glares at Wicked Willie, and Sidney Sly the stoat.
Each one cannot speak, as there's a frog in each one's throat.
"I should banish you to Sadland, but as Carnival is here,
I will cast a magic spell which will last a fairy year".

She waves her magic wand. First a flash! and then a pop!
Poor Wicked Willie tries to run, but he can only hop.
Sly Sidney starts to laugh at Mary's funny joke,

But the laugh's on him as from his throat
comes a very froggy croak!
Both Willie and Sly Sidney have turned a
ghastly green,
With bulging eyes like saucers, they squat
before their queen.

"I've turned you into frogs, as you've made me
hopping mad!
So. Hop to it! Clean up this shop, in return for
being bad.
And any other duties that you are told to do,
you'll jump to them right away, if you know
what's good for you."
Suddenly, they try to leap in the direction of
the door,
but Prickles Sharp grabs their froggy legs and
gives them both what for.
"Look before you leap, my lads, or I will make
you holler.
I will lead you everywhere, and both of you I'll
collar."
He leads them sharply with a pull around Roy
Rabbit's shop.
They jump to it right away, cleaning up
without a stop.
Mary leaves them with a sigh; "It's sad that
they've done wrong.

But it's only for a fairy year which isn't very long."

Robway

CARNIVAL MORNING

Moon has gone to sleep. Night has crept away,
Sun has risen from his bed to start another day.
Scurry Skylark's calling as he rises in the sky.
He is an early bird and a happy bird, but why?
"Wake up everybody; wake up and be gay!
Don't just lie there in your beds, today's a
holiday."
Fairies stretch their wings and rub their tired
eyes.
Who is this busy body, shouting from the
skies?

Now Pigeon Post is calling. He's another early
bird,
Delivering written letters and messages by
word.
He's holding up the mail, with talented sharp
claws.
He never drops a single note, except through
noted doors.

A circular tour a day of constant to and froing,
Does wonders for his pigeon brain, keeping
circulation going.
Today his bag is bulging with envelopes
galore.

He drops a message through each box, and
coos at every door.

As he's a homing bird, his job is always fun.
Each time he flies around he gets a pigeon hole
in one.
Owners of a letter-box with dirty marks and
smears
Will receive, delivered for free, a box around
the ears.

But today is Carnival Day and there are cards
for all.
Mary, the Queen of Fairy Glade, requests your
company at the ball.

PREPARING FOR THE GREAT DAY

All scamper to the stream to take their morning
dip.
Cow-slips in her hurry, head first without a
slip.
They wish to look their best for the carnival
today,
So, they preen and plume and primp
themselves.
What a fine display!

A contest has been planned to find a pretty
maid,
Who is also kind and gentle, the best in Fairy
Glade.
She will travel to the ball with bold Sir Grassy
Hopper.
He's so handsome and so proud in his shiny
coal-black topper.
It's a very special honour, and maids jump at
such a chance,
Being partner to Sir Hopper at Mary's special
dance.
Wish Fish will be busy, for everyone today
Will wish to look their best. He'll wish they'd
go away.

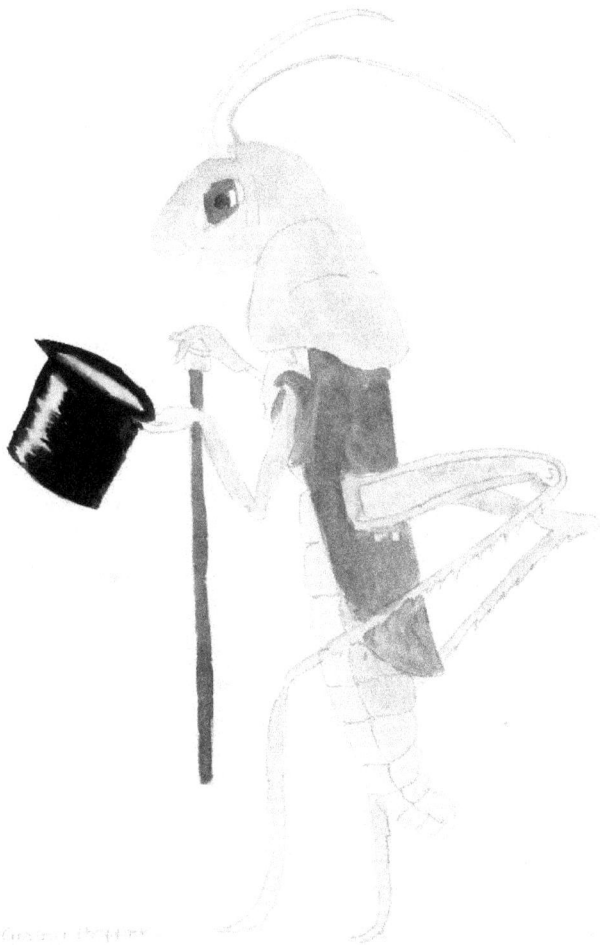

WITCHITY WILDCAT

Witchity Wildcat is fierce and mean,
The wildest cat Fairy Glade has seen
He prowls on the edge of Dingle Dell
Waiting to pounce near Wish Fish's well.
Knees start to knock at the sight of this cat
Prowling and pouncing and knocking all flat.
Sprightly springing on whoever falls prey,
Whoever comes cat's catastrophical way.

Fairies and all go in twos and threes
Whenever they venture near Dingle Dell trees.
But he leaps onto fairies and all who pass by,
Making them scream and start to cry.
He bristles his hairs and arches his back.
With his striking tail, giving each a whack.
His whiskers quiver at the thought of meat,
Good fairies and all are good things to eat.

Sensible fairies fly very high, as cat cannot
reach them up in the sky.
But, fairies get tired at the end of the day,
After beating their wings such a fairy long
way.
So Witchity waits in a witch-elm tree
And grabs them really quick, before they can
flee.

He seizes and teases with gaping jaws.
Scritching and scratching with glistening
claws.

Spitting and spatting, baring his teeth,
Making them shiver and shake like a leaf.
It's wicked and mean of Witchity Cat
Doing such naughty things as that.
When fairies and all are tucked up in bed,
His eerie howls fill them with dread.
Legs turn to jelly - hearts pound with fright
As Witchity's caterwauls wail through the
night.

Each has good reason to be filled with fear,
As they know, that he knows, the contest is
near.
He's calling to them: "I'm waiting for you
If you visit Wish-Fish for a wish to come true!"

MORRIS MOLE

Poor Morris Mole is as blind as a bat.
He has short hairy legs and is very fat.
He builds all the houses round about,
Which should be square, without a doubt.
His ceilings slope towards the floor,
Which happens a lot, when your eyesight's
poor,
And you can't see the plans in front of you
And you stick with syrup instead of glue.

Smoke curls up through the chimney stack
And then curls down on the long journey back.
For, when Mr. Mole saw the weathervane,
He blocked up the chimney, in case it should
rain.
Press down a switch to turn on the light
And you're sure to be in for a bit of a fright.
If Morris Mole has built your home,
You'll get a quick bath with plenty of foam.

There are three legs on the four-legged chairs
And he forgot the steps in the wooden stairs.
So, unless you're a fairy, who flies to her sleep,
You'd best be a frog, who enjoys a good leap.
He has lots on his mind, so he isn't to blame
If he forgets to put glass in the window-frame,

And what if he has forgotten the door?
There's not many could make such mistakes
galore.

But Morris is happy as he trundles along.
Whistling a tune, or singing a song.
Did you ever see such a cheerful soul
As our dear short-sighted Morris Mole?
And his houses are friendly - look over there!
The walls give a wave and the windows don't
glare.
Each raises its roof in a well-mannered way.
No, there's no place like home, not on Carnival
Day!

The stage is all set. It's built good and strong.
Of course, Mr. Mole has helped it along.
But, round-about houses are no guarantee
That Morris's stage won't get stage fright and
flee.

SALLY SILKWORM & CO

Sally Silkworm's busy in her working den,
Spinning with her spinneret, with help from
Jenny Wren.
They love to spin a yarn and never lose the
thread,
Material is chosen well as Sally is well bred.
As Sally spins the silk, Jenny weaves it into
cloth,
Then takes it to the cocoon home of Silky Sat-in
Moth.
Moth spreads it out to dry on a tasty mulberry
leaf.
Then happily cuts it into shape, with
crunching, munching teeth.

Miss Caterpillar helps to sew each satin stitch.
Inch Worm measures everyone to see there is
no hitch.
Snail glides back and forth, giving one last
press.
Mayflies spin and whirl around, showing off
each dress.
Everyone today will want a nice new gown,
They come to Silky Sat-in Moth's, as she's the
best in town!

GLORIA GLOWORM
LIGHT-HOUSE KEEPER

"I'm Gloria Glowworm. I sell fairy lights
In my bright little shop, for the darkest of
nights.
I'll welcome you in with a warm shining smile.
Don't glow too soon. Please! Stay for a while!

Switch to my lights, quite safe, but not dear.
My shades are pure crystal, fluorescent and
clear.
Don't buy in Sadland. Black Witch sells there,
Dim shades of darkness and lamps of despair.

My lamps warn of danger. They flicker and
fade,
If you happen to fit a deadly-night-shade.
It's almost midday. The contest's at noon.
I must shut up shop and get ready quite soon.

I'll win first prize, of course, you can tell
In my bright, light green dress that suits me so
well.
I've lots of admirers. Look around and you'll
see
A shop full of moths all attracted to me.

Please call again. You know what they say.
Gloria Glowworm will brighten your day."

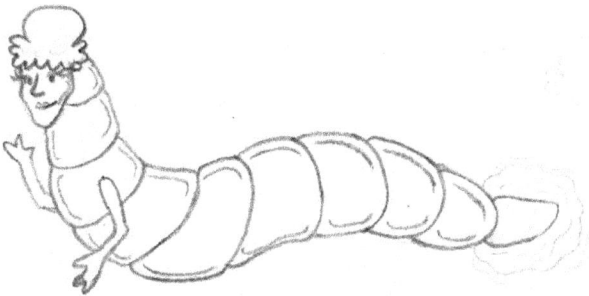

RAGGED ROBIN

Poor Ragged Robin comes into town,
Dragging her wings, her head hanging down.
No note does she sing from her sweet little
throat,
But a chorus is heard as cruel fairies gloat.
"It's little Miss Ragged, so spotty and brown.
So dull and so dowdy in her raggedy gown!"

Her mother keeps saying, "Don't worry, some
day,
You'll wake and you'll find your spots gone
away.
Just pray with your heart and wish with your
mind
For a beautiful gown of a deep rosy kind."
Thinks Ragged Miss Robin, "I hope mummy's
right.
I'm fed up with being this horrible sight!"

It's Carnival Day. She wakes with a start.
She's wished and she's prayed so hard from
her heart.
She hops from her bed to the mirror and there
Staring back is a maid so lovely and fair,
In a beautiful gown. No spots to be seen.
The rosiest red that a gown's ever been.

"Oh, my!" sings Miss Robin and laughs with such glee.
"Is it true looking-glass? Is this maid really me!?"
"Oh yes!" says the mirror. "You were promised one day
If you're true, good and kind, then your spots fade away.
So, go into town and there you will find
All who look at you, most gracious and kind."

So, off sets sweet Robin, to town, once more.
No longer dragging her wings as before.
Her eyes sparkle brightly, her head held up high.
She's feeling so happy, she sings to the sky.
All who look on her are dazed by her charms.
"Look at Miss Robin!" they wave with their arms.

A chorus begins. The cruel fairies gloat.
"Look!" but the words get stuck in their throat.
"It's little Miss Ragged. Or is it?" they say.
There's no dowdy dress and all spots gone away.
She's lovely and fair in her beautiful gown.
They hate to admit, the best in town!

THE CONTEST

The Judges assemble. What a job they have
got.
I don't think, they thought, they'd get such a
lot.
A number is placed on each entry maid,
As they stand in line for the big parade.

The compere is Freddie, that artful young fox.
He's so crafty and sly, but a smooth chatterbox.
Maids trip on the stage with a nervous frown,
As Freddie has chased every bird in town.

He rubs his hands and smiles with glee
As he thinks about what he'd like for tea.
Both Swallow and Swift start flapping their
praise
As they follow each maid on the stage with
their gaze.

Woodpecker Tapper forgets himself too,
And in his excitement, pecks his chair through.
Boring Wilf Woodworm is too tired to peep,
So, he bores a hole, crawls in it and promptly
falls asleep.

Bashful Badger is blushing and covers his eyes.

"Oh dear"! he exclaims and "What a surprise!"
He's usually asleep at this time in his bed,
But, today is so special, he's come here instead.

Miss Gloria Glowworm leads the way.
She's so very sure she'll win today.
Following her is Marguerite.
Followed and followed by Milly Pede's feet.

Coming up now is Daisy and May.
I really must say, they're happy and gay.
And Hazel Nut, she's very funny,
Cracking jokes with Binny Bunny.

Gardenia is strutting by
with glamorous Gladys Gladioli.
Erica Earwig crawls behind
sweet Rosemary, who's sweet and kind.
Here comes pretty Polly Pansy
and poor Miss clumsy try-hard Tansy
As she tries to quicken her pace,
she trips and falls flat on her face.

As Ragged Robin takes the floor,
cheers go up with a shout and a roar.
She's so pretty and neat and graceful as well.
They've never seen her look so swell.
Heads all go a 'bibbin' and a 'bobbin'

When they see this 'not so' Ragged Robin.

Dashing up is Bizzie Lizzie
 with crumpled dress and hair so frizzy.
Flora-Bunda fairy's flying past.
 With that speed she won't be last.
Tingaling ting comes Miss Bluebell.
  She's run all the way from Dingle Dell.
Following her is Bittersweet.
  She's a two-faced thing and a bit of a cheat.

Fingers in ears is Periwinkle Pixie,
trying not to listen to Tell-tale Trixie.
Miss Myrtle Moth goes flitting by,
catching up Miss Damsel Fly.
Daffodilly and Diffodally are
side by side Miss Lily-of-the-valley.
Well! What a contest this will be.
 Who will win? You wait and see.

DISASTER STRIKES THE STAGE

Morris Mole cannot see. See how hard though he tries
Wiping his glasses and rubbing his eyes.
He thought it clever to bring a sharp pin
And a list of names to stick it in.

He misses the list. Then, straight and true.
The pin goes into - can you guess who?!
Prickles Sharp Cop lets out a yell.
"Arrest that mole! I'm not feeling well!

Get me a doctor! Get me a nurse!
He's a public nuisance and what's worse,
It's a wonder to me if this stage will survive
And these maids all get off in one piece and alive."

Oh no! Prickles Sharp. Do not say things like that!
"Too late!" says the stage. "I'm feeling quite flat."
With a crick and a crack. With a grunt and a groan.
The floor of the stage takes a break with a moan.

The weight on his back is too much to bare

So, he tugs and he shrugs, throwing all in the air.
They tipple and topple. They scream and they shout.
They don't look so nice, upside down, roundabout.

THE WINNER IS CHOSEN

The judges have chosen, before the melee,
the maid that has won, on this Carnival day.
Freddy shouts "Order! The voting is done.
We're about to announce the one that has won.

The one that has won and is Maid of the Glade!
The kindest and best in this big parade
Is Miss Ragged Robin!"
"Hoorah!" they all yell. Such clapping! Such
cheering! Such stamping as well!

"Oh my!" says Miss Robin. "Oh my and oh
me!
Thank you! Oh, thank you!" she warbles with
glee
She flickers and flutters her tail and her wings.
Her heart is so happy. She heartily sings.

Queen Mary smiles sweetly. "Well done, little
maid."
And crowns the young robin Miss Maid of the
Glade!
In her dainty red dress, she parades all around.
Proud pretty Robin is so glad to be crowned.

TO THE BALL

As the Golden Coach pulls up near the stage
with six white horses, a coachman and page,
Sir Hopper alights. "I'm yours for the day.
Let's go to the ball!" And they ride away.

They dance for five days, and they dance for
five nights,
to daffodil trumpets and Peter Pan pipes.
Yes! A wonderful time is had by all!
At Queen Mary Fairy's Annual Ball

GOODBYE TO HAPPYLAND

It's time to go home, so wish for your bed.
And when you wake up you'll be there
instead.
But please come again, on a fine, sunny day,
As Happyland's only a bubble away.

About the Author

Gilly is a popular poet and singer, who is much in demand around East Anglia. She was born in Marlow to an accountant father who loved to write stories and poems, and a mother who, before her marriage, had been a piano teacher.

Gilly attended High Wycombe High School, where the teachers loved her poems which she had been writing since early childhood. An early one featured a gorilla.

She moved to this area in the sixties and wrote poems about events in her life and was also a singer in a Caister folk group. Gradually she began to write comedy but also tackles more serious subjects.

Singing is very important to Gilly, who was the best singer in her first year of high school and has been known to sing in as many as four choirs at once.

She is still singing and reciting her poems to appreciative audiences.

Gilly now lives in Lowestoft.